PRISCILA JUNE

GIFTS OF IMPERFECTION

The Ultimate Guide to Overcoming Your Imperfections,
Learn How to Take Action And Believe In Yourself
Despite the Imperfections

Descrierea CIP a Bibliotecii Naţionale a României
PRISCILA JUNE
   GIFTS OF IMPERFECTION. The Ultimate Guide to
Overcoming Your Imperfections, Learn How to Take Action
And Believe In Yourself Despite the Imperfections / Priscila
June. – Bucharest: Editura My Ebook, 2020
   ISBN

PRISCILA JUNE

GIFTS OF IMPERFECTION

The Ultimate Guide to Overcoming Your Imperfections, Learn How to Take Action And Believe In Yourself Despite the Imperfections

My Ebook Publishing House
Bucharest, 2020

TABLE OF CONTENTS

FOREWORD

Unconsciously we're forming habits each moment of our lives. A few are habits of a worthy nature; some are those of a most unpleasant nature. A few, though not so bad in themselves, are extremely bad in their cumulative effects, and cause us from time to time much loss, much pain and anguish, while their inverses would, contrarily, bring as a great deal of peace and joy, as well as a continually increasing power.

Have we it inside our power to determine at all times what sorts of habits shall take form in our lives? Put differently, is habit-forming, character building, a matter of simple chance, or have we it inside our own control? We have, totally and utterly. "I will be what I will to be," may be said and ought to be said by each human soul. After this has been bravely and unfalteringly stated, and not only stated, but fully inwardly recognized, something yet remains.

Something remains to be stated regarding the excellent law underlying habit-forming, character building; for there's a simple, natural, and soundly scientific method that all ought to know. A method whereby old, unsuitable, earth-binding ways of thinking may be broken, and fresh, desirable, heaven lifting thoughts can be acquired, a process whereby life in part or in its totality may be changed, provided one is sufficiently in earnest to know and, knowing it, to use it.

Taking Action In Spite Of Imperfection

*How To Break Through Analytical Constipation
And Paralysis In Order To Get Things Done Even If
Things Are Imperfect!*

CHAPTER 1

OUR MIND

Synopsis

Thought is the drive implicit in all. And what do we mean by this? Merely this: Your every act - each conscious act - is premised by a thought.

Your commanding thoughts influence your dominating actions. In the domain of our own brains we have total control, or we ought to have, and if at any time we haven't, then there's a technique by which we may gain control, and in the domain of the brain become thorough masters.

In order to get to the real foundation of the matter, let us look to this for a minute. For if thought is forever parent to our acts, habits, character, life, then it's first essential that we know totally how to command our thoughts.

Our Thoughts

Here let us refer to the law of the brain which is the same as is the law in association with the reflex nerve system of the body, the law which states that whenever one does a particular thing in a particular way it's easier to do the same thing in the same way the following time, and still simpler the next, and the next, and the next, till in time it comes to pass that no work is required, or no work worth speaking of; but on the opposite would call for the effort.

The brain carries with it the might that perpetuates its own sort of thought, the same as the body carries with it through the reflex nerve system the might which perpetuates and makes continually easier its own specific acts. Thus a easy effort to control one's thoughts, a easy setting about it, even if initially failure is the outcome, and even if for a time failure appears to be about the sole result, will in time, eventually, bring him to the point of simple, full, and complete command.

Each one, then, may grow the power of determining, commanding his thought, the power of determining what sorts of thought he shall and what sorts he shall not entertain.

For let us never part in mind with this reality, that each earnest effort along any line makes the end aimed at simply a little easier for every succeeding effort, even if, as has been stated, apparent failure is the outcome of the earlier efforts. This is a case where even failure is success, for the failure isn't in the effort, and each sincere effort adds an increment of might that will finally achieve the end aimed at. We may, then, gain the full and utter power of determining what character, what sort of thoughts we think of.

Shall we now provide attention to a concrete example? Here is a gentleman, the cashier of a big sales outlet, or cashier of a bank. In his morning newspaper he reads of a man who's become suddenly wealthy, has made a fortune of half a million or a million dollars in a couple of hours through speculation on the stock exchange. Maybe he's seen an account of a different gentleman who's done practically the same thing recently.

He is not quite judicious enough, however, to understand the fact that when he reads of one or two cases of this sort he may find, were he to look into the matter cautiously, one or two hundred cases of gentlemen who have lost all they had in the same way.

He believes, however, that he will be among the fortunate ones. He doesn't fully recognize that there are no short cuts to wealth realistically made.

He takes a part of his nest egg, and as is true in practically all cases of this sort, he loses all that he's put in, thinking now that he sees why he lost, and that if he had more cash he would be able to get back what he's lost, and maybe make a handsome sum in addition, and make it rapidly, the thought comes to him to utilize some of the funds he has charge of.

In 9 cases out of 10, if not 10 cases in every 10, the results that inescapably follow this are known sufficiently well to make it hard for him to continue.

Where is the man's safety in the light of what we have been thinking about? Merely this: the moment the thought of utilizing

14

for his own purpose funds belonging to other people enters his mind, if he's wise he will at once put the thought from his mind.

If he's a fool he will think of it. In the degree in which he thinks of it, it will grow on him; it will become the engrossing thought in his brain; it will finally become master of his self-control, and through quickly succeeding steps, dishonor, shame, and degradation, penitentiary, remorse will be his.

It's simple for him to put the thought from his brain when it first enters; but as he thinks of it, it grows to such proportions that it becomes more and more hard for him to put it from his mind; and later it becomes practically impossible for him to do it.

The light of the match, which but a little effort of the breath would have snuffed it initially, has imparted a flame that's raging through the whole building, and now it's almost if not rather impossible to subdue it.

CHAPTER 2

HOW BELIEFS BEGIN

Synopsis

Shall we note a different case? A trite case, maybe, but one in which we may see how belief is formed, and also how the same belief may be unformed.

Here is a fellow, he might be the son of poor parents, or he might be the son of rich parents; one in the average ranks of life, or one of high societal standing, whatever that means. He's good hearted, one of great impulses broadly speaking, a good fellow.

He's out with some associates, companions of the same common type. They're out for a pleasant evening, out for a great time. They're apt at times to be uncaring, even thoughtless.

The proposition is made by one of the company, not that they get intoxicated, no, not at all; but simply that they go and have something to drink together. Now what happens?

How It Happens

The fellow whom we firstly mentioned, desiring to be genial, barely listens to the suggestion that comes into his inner consciousness that it will be better for him not to fall in with the other people in this. He doesn't stop long enough to recognize the fact that the greatest potency and nobility of character lies always in admitting a firm stand on the side of the right, and let himself be influenced by nothing that will undermine this stand.

He goes, consequently, with his companions to the drinking place. With the same or with additional companions this is duplicated from time to time; and every time it's repeated his might of saying "No" is gradually diminishing. In this way he's grown a little liking for alcohol, and takes it perhaps at times by himself.

He doesn't dream, or in the slightest degree recognize, what way he's tending, till there comes a day when he wakes up to the awareness of the fact that he hasn't the might nor even the impulse to resist the taste which has bit by bit grown into a minor sort of craving for alcohol. Thinking, all the same, that he will be able to quit when he's truly in danger of getting into the drink habit, he goes unthinkingly and heedlessly on.

We'll skip the various steps and come to the time when we find him a confirmed drunk. It's merely the same old story told a 1000 or even a 1000000 times over.

He at last wakes up to his real condition; and through the disgrace, the anguish, the degradation, and the want that comes across him he longs for a return of the days when he was a free man. But hope has nearly gone from his life. It would have been simpler for him never to have started, and easier for him to have stopped before he achieved his present condition; but even in his current condition, be it the humblest and the most helpless and hopeless that may be imagined, he's the power to get out of it and be a free man again.

Let us see. The want for drink falls upon him again. If he flirts with the thought, the want, he's lost again. His only hope, his only means of evasion is this: the moment, uh-huh, the very minute the thought comes to him, if he will put it out of his brain he will thereby smother the little flame of the match.

If he flirts with the thought the little flame will communicate itself till almost before he's aware of it an overwhelming fire is raging, and then effort is almost worthless. The thought has to be banished from the brain the instant it enters; dawdling with it means failure and defeat, or a battle that will be unspeakably fiercer than it would be if the thought is booted out at the beginning.

And here we have to say a word regarding a particular thing that we might call the "natural of indirectness." A thought may be put out of the brain easier and more successfully, not by dwelling on it, not by, trying to put it out directly, but by throwing the brain on to another object by putting another object of thought into the brain. This might be, for instance, the ideal of full and perfect self-mastery, or it might be something of a nature totally distinct from the idea which presents itself, something to which the brain goes easily and naturally.

This will eventually become the engrossing thought in the brain, and the danger is past. This same course repeated will bit by bit grow the power of putting more readily out of brain the thought of drink as it exhibits itself, and will bit by bit grow the power of putting into the brain those objects of thought one most wants.

The result will be that as time passes the idea of drink will present itself less and less, and when it does exhibit itself it may be put out of the brain more easily each succeeding time, till the time comes when it may be put out without trouble, and finally the time will come when the thought will enter the brain no longer at all.

CHAPTER 3

THE POWER OF MANIFESTATION

Synopsis

Still a different case: You might be roughly of an irritable nature by nature, maybe, aggravated easily to anger. Somebody says something or does something that you dislike, and your beginning impulse is to show gall and possibly to fall into anger.

In the degree that you let this resentment display itself, that you let yourself cave in to anger, in this degree will it become simpler to do the same thing when any cause, even a really slight cause, exhibits itself.

It will, furthermore, become continually more difficult for you to refrain from it, till resentment, anger, and possibly even hate and revenge become features of your nature, robbing it of its brightness, its appeal, and its warmth for all with whom you come in contact.

We can manifest what we wish.

Drawing What We Choose

If, all the same, the split second the impulse to bitterness and anger arises, you arrest it then and there, and throw the brain on to another object of thought, the might will gradually grow itself of executing this same thing more promptly, more easily, as future like causes exhibit themselves, till later the time will come when there will be barely anything that may irritate you, and nothing that may impel you to angriness; till later a unmatched brightness and appeal of nature and temperament will become routinely yours, a brightness and appeal you'd barely think possible nowadays.

And so we may take up case after case, feature after feature, habit after habit. The habit of faultfinding and its contrary are grown in identically the same way; the feature of jealousy and its inverse; the feature of dread and its inverse. In that same way we develop either love or hate; in that way we come to take a blue, pessimistic view of life, which objectifies itself in a nature, a inclination of this sort, or we grow that cheery, hopeful, upbeat, perky nature that brings with it such joy and beauty and power for ourselves, as well as so much promise and inspiration and joy for all the cosmos.

There's nothing more truthful in connection with human life than that we grow into the semblance of those matters we contemplate. Literally and scientifically and inevitably true is it that "as a man thinketh in his heart, so is he." The "is" part is his nature. His nature is the sum of his beliefs. His beliefs have been forged by· his witting acts; but each witting act is, as we have discovered, preceded by a thought. And so we have it - belief on the one hand, nature, life, and destiny on the other. And easy it becomes when we bear in mind that it's merely the thought of the here and now, and the next minute when it's upon us, and then the following, and so forth through all time. One may in this way arrive at whatever ideals he would arrive at. 2 steps are essential:

- ❑ 1st, as the days pass, to form one's ideals; and
- ❑ 2nd, to follow them continually, whatever might come up, wherever they might lead him.

Forever remember that the great and strong character is the one who's ever ready to sacrifice the current pleasure for the future good. He who will therefore follow his highest ideals as they exhibit themselves to him day in day out, year after year, will find that eventually he will be at the gates of paradise.

Life isn't, we might say, for simple passing pleasure, but for the greatest unfolding that one may aspire to, the noblest character that one may develop, and for the highest service that one may render to all humanity. In that, however, we'll discover the highest pleasure, for in this the only real pleasure lies. He who would come across it by any short cuts, or by lucking into any other paths, will inevitably discover that his last state is always worse than his first; and if he go along paths other than these he will discover that he will never find true and lasting pleasure in the least.

CHAPTER 4

OUR CIRCUMSTANCES

Synopsis

The question isn't, "What are the circumstances in our lives?" but, "How do we converge the circumstances that we find there?"

And whatever the circumstances are, it's unwise and unprofitable to think of them, even if they're circumstances that we'd have otherwise, in the attitude of complaint, for complaint will bring natural depression, and depression will dampen and possibly even kill the spirit that would spawn the power that would enable us to impart into our lives an altogether new set of circumstances.

Responding

In order to be concrete, even at the risk of becoming personal, I'll state that there have come at assorted times into my life conditions and circumstances that I gladly would have escaped from at the time-conditions that induced at the time mortification and shame and torture of spirit.

But invariably, as sufficient time has blew over, I - or anybody for that matter - have been able to review and see clearly the part that each experience of the sort just mentioned had to play out in my life.

I've seen the lessons it was crucial for me to learn; and the result is that now I would not drop one of these things from my life, demeaning and hard to bear as they were at the time; no, not for the world.

And here is likewise a lesson I've learned: whatever circumstances are in my life now that are not the simplest and most agreeable, and whatever circumstances of this sort all coming time might bring, I'll take them just as they come, without complaint, without natural depression, and meet them in the most judicious possible way; knowing that they're the best possible circumstances that could be in my life at the time, or otherwise they wouldn't be there.

I recognized the fact that, while I might not at the time see why they're in my life, although I might not see just what part they have to play, the time will come, and when it comes I'll see it all, and thank the higher power for each condition just as it came.

Each one is so given to think that his own circumstances, his own trials or hassles or grief, or his own battles, as the case might be, are heavier than those of the great mass of humanity or possibly greater than those of anybody else in the world. He blanks out that each one has his own special trials or problems or grief to bear, or battles to defeat, and that his is but the general lot of all mankind.

We're apt to make the error in this - in that we see and feel keenly our own trials, or inauspicious circumstances, or characteristics to be overpowered, while those of others we don't see so clearly and hence we're apt to believe that they're not at all equal to our own. Each has his own issues to solve.

Each must solve his own jobs. Each must grow the perceptiveness that will enable him to see what the causes are that have brought the unfavorable circumstances into his life; each must grow the potency that will enable him to face these circumstances, and to set into operation forces that will manifest a different set of circumstances.

We might be of aid to each other by way of suggestion, by way of bringing to each other a knowledge of particular higher laws and forces - laws and forces that will make it simpler to accomplish that which we would accomplish. The executing, however, must be done by each one for himself.

And so the way to leave of any circumstance we have got into, either wittingly or unknowingly, either by choice or accidentally is to take time to look the circumstances squarely in the face, and to discover the law whereby they've happened.

And when we have discovered the law, the thing to do is not to rise up against it, not to reject it, but to go with it by working in harmony with it.

When we work in harmony with it, it will work for our greatest good, and will take us wherever we want. If we fight it, if we balk it, if we fail to work in harmony with it, it will finally break us to pieces.

The law is changeless in its workings. Go with it, and it brings all matters our way; balk it, and it brings agony, pain, loss, and loneliness.

CHAPTER 5

TAKING ACTION

Synopsis

Belief is at the bottom of all advancement or retrogression, of all success or failure, of all that's suitable or unsuitable in human life. The sort of thought we think of both produces and draws circumstances that crystallize about it, circumstances exactly the same in nature as is the thought that affords them form.

Thoughts are forces, and each creates of its kind, whether we recognize it or not. The great law, which states that like produces like, and that like draws in like, is continually working in each human life, for it's one of the great changeless laws of the cosmos.

Some Insight

For one to take time to see distinctly the things he would achieve to, and then to hold that ideal steady and continually before his brain, never allowing faith - his favorable thought-forces - to give way to or to be counteracted by doubts and dreads, and then to set about doing every day what his hands find to accomplish, never complaining, but spending the time that he would differently spend in complaint in centering his thought- forces on the ideal that his brain has built, will eventually bring about the full manifestation of that for which he sets out.

There are those who, when they start to grasp the fact that there is what we might term a "science of thought," who, when they start to recognize that through the instrumentality of our inner, spiritual, thought-forces we have the might of gradually molding the daily conditions of life as we would have them, in their early exuberance are not able to see results as rapidly as they expect and are liable to think, therefore, that after all there is not a great deal in that which has but newly come to their understanding. They have to remember, however, that in striving to overcome some thoughts or to grow a new belief, everything can't be done all of a sudden.

In the degree that we set about to utilize the thought-forces do we continually become able to utilize them more effectively. Progress is slow initially, speedier as we continue. Power grows by utilizing, or, put differently, utilizing brings a continually increasing might. This is regulated by law the same as are all matters in our lives, and all matters in the cosmos about us. Each act and advancement is in full accordance with law.

No one embarking on the study of music may, for instance, sit down to the piano and play a masterpiece initially. He must not conclude, however, nor does he conclude, that the piece can't be played by him, or, for that matter, by anybody. He starts to practice the piece.

The law of the brain that we have already noticed comes to his aid, whereby his brain follows the music more readily, more speedily, and more surely every succeeding time, and there likewise comes into operation and to his aid the law underlying the action of the reflexive nerve system of the body, which we have likewise noticed, whereby his hands co-ordinate their movements with the movements of his brain more promptly, more speedily, and more accurately every succeeding time; till later the time comes when that which he stumbles through initially, that in which there's no harmony, nothing but discord, at last reveals itself as the music of the master, the music that thrills and moves masses . It's in the use of the thought-forces. It's the reiteration, the constant reduplication of the thought that grows the might of continually stronger thought-focusing, and that ultimately brings manifestation.

There's character building not only for the young but for the old also. And what a difference there is in elderly individuals! How many grow old graciously, and how many grow old in ways of rather a different nature.

There's a sweetness and charm that combine for attractiveness in old age the same as there is something that can't be identified by these words. A few grow continually more dear to their acquaintances and to the members of their immediate families, while others get possessed of the idea that their acquaintances and the members of their families have less of a regard for them than they once had, and many times they're not far wrong. The one continually sees more in life to like, the other sees continually less. The one becomes more dear and magnetic to other people, the other less so.

And why is this? By chance? Not by a long sight. Personally I don't believe there's any such thing as chance in the whole of human life, nor even in the world or the great universe in which we exist. The one great law of cause and effect is conclusive; and effect is always akin to its own special cause, although we might have at times to go back considerably farther than we're accustomed to in order to discover the cause, the parent of this or that effect, or actualized, though not necessarily permanently actualized, condition.

Why, then, the huge difference in the 2 types of elderly individuals? The one keeps from torments, and fear, and fret, and foundationless imaginings, while the other appears particularly to cultivate these, to give himself or herself particularly to them. And why is this? At a particular time in life, differing slightly in different people, life-long mental states, beliefs, and characteristics start to focus themselves and come to the surface, as it were. Predominating thoughts and mental states start to show themselves in actualized characters and features as never before, and no one is immune. If one would develop a beautiful and magnetic old age, he has to start it in youth and in middle life. If, however, he's neglected or failed in this, he may then wisely conform himself to conditions and give himself zealously to putting into operation all essential counter-balancing forces and influences. Where there's life nothing is ever irretrievably lost, though the enjoyment of the higher good might be long delayed.

Wrapping Up

The life of every one is in his own hands and he may make it in character, in attainment, in power, in divine self-fulfillment, and hence in influence, exactly what he wills to make it. All matters that he most fondly dreams of are his, or might become so if he's truly in earnest; and as he rises more and more to his ideal, and grows in the strength and influence of his nature, he becomes an illustration and an inspiration to all with whom he comes in contact; so that through him the weak and faltering are encouraged and fortified; so that those of low ideals and of a low type of life instinctively and inescapably have their ideals raised, and the ideals of no one may be raised without its showing forth in his outer life.

As he advances in his grasp on and understanding of the power and strength of the thought-forces, he discovers that a lot of times through the process of mental suggestion he may be of tremendous aid to one who's weak and fighting, by sending him at times, and by continually holding him in, the highest thought, in the thought of the highest strength, wisdom and love. The might of "suggestion," mental suggestion, is one that has enormous possibilities for good if we'll but study it carefully, comprehend it fully, and utilize it justly.

Printed by Libri Plureos GmbH in Hamburg, Germany